Very
PESTO

Very PESTO

DOROTHY RANKIN

CELESTIAL ARTS
Berkeley | Toronto

Celestial Arts
P. O. Box 7123
Berkeley, California 94707
www.tenspeed.com

Distributed in Australia by Simon and Schuster Australia, in Canada by Ten Speed Press Canada, in New Zealand by Southern Publishers Group, in South Africa by Real Books, and in the United Kingdom and Europe by Airlift Book Company.

Cover design by Nancy Austin and Chloe Rawlins based on an original design by Susanne Weihl
Text design by Chloe Rawlins based on an original design by Susanne Weihl

Library of Congress Cataloging-in-Publication Data
Rankin, Dottie.
   Very pesto / Dorothy Rankin. — [Rev. ed.]
     p. cm.
   Rev. ed. of: Pestos! Trumansburg, NY : Crossing Press, c1985.
   ISBN 1-58761-208-9 (pbk.)
   1. Pestos. I. Rankin, Dottie. Pestos! II. Title.

   TX819.P45R38 2004
   641.8'14—dc22   2004006119

First printing, 2004
Printed in Singapore

1 2 3 4 5 6 7 8 9 10 — 08 07 06 05 04

To my mother, Mary, and all the Packards,
who sure knew how to cook.

Acknowledgments

*My thanks go to family and friends who enabled me to stay with this project:
Laurie Pettibon, for her creative ideas, unwavering support, and
invaluable input; Andrea Chesman, editor and friend, for her guidance,
faith, and encouragement; Linda Mansfield, for her enthusiasm and support;
Patty Brushett, whose friendship means so much; and Amy Moody,
favorite foodie and friend who makes it fun.*

Contents

INTRODUCTION   1

HERB PESTOS   8

PASTA AND PESTOS   28

FOR OPENERS: APPETIZERS, SALADS,
   AND BREADS   44

SIDES AND ENTRÉES   74

Introduction

It is said, "He who eats pesto never leaves Genoa."

A Genoese pesto is undoubtedly one of the world's great culinary pleasures. Made from fresh basil leaves, pale green oil from ripe olives, a local sharp sheep's cheese, garlic, and pine nuts, this sublime essence is especially savored during the lush summer months.

In Genoa, where pesto originated, fresh basil is available year-round. The word *pesto*, derives from the Italian *pesto* meaning "pounded." Today, the food processor and blender have replaced the mortar and pestle and the freezer has made it possible to store quantities of pesto for enjoyment year-round.

The variables in a classic basil pesto are many. There are no givens when it comes to making pestos in Genoa or in other provinces of Italy. No two towns make it the same way. Some versions include cream, other pestos call for butter. Pine nuts (pignolia) are a later addition to pesto. A Genoese pesto may contain all Sardo pecorino cheese (made from sheep's milk), whereas in this country, we usually combine a Romano pecorino and Parmesan cheese or make a pesto with all Parmesan. As Ed Giobbi said in his book *Italian Family Cooking*, "When I was in Genoa, I tried to find the truly authentic version [of pesto], but that experience convinced me that there is no such thing."

This book contains a very classic version of pesto and recipes that use the pesto as a seasoning. There are also some rather unusual pestos, using such diverse herbs as cilantro, rosemary, mint, and oregano thyme. I hope that these recipes will be used as suggestions and inspirations for cooking with herbs.

INGREDIENTS
Making herb pestos definitely begins with selecting quality ingredients.

Herbs Remove the stems and lightly pack the leaves in a measuring cup. Measure before you wash. To wash the leaves, immerse them in a bowl of cold water and swish them around. Drain in a strainer or colander and roll gently in a towel, or spin dry in a salad spinner. Fluff up the leaves and spread them on towels to dry further as you prepare the other ingredients.

Garlic Good fresh garlic is an integral component of this queen of sauces. Elephant garlic can be used; but since its flavor is considerably milder than garlic, adjust the number of cloves. The fresher the garlic, the better the flavor.

Cheese Next, the cheese is added to the pesto. It must be freshly grated for full flavor. Buy the cheese in a chunk and grate it by hand or in a food processor, first with the grating disk, then the steel blade. I freeze extra grated cheese in small containers. Stored this way, grated cheese will retain its fresh flavor for up to 6 weeks.

Since Italian Sardo pecorino is hard to find, a blend of freshly grated Parmesan and Romano pecorino seems to provide the best combination of sharpness and mellow flavor.

Asiago cheese works well in a mild-flavored pesto, such as Lemon Pesto (page 15) or Tarragon Pesto (page 21).

Oil The choice of the right oil is most important in pesto. A virgin olive oil, defined as a second-press oil, should provide sufficient quality. The strong flavor of the pesto overpowers the fruity extra virgin olive oil, although it will certainly make a fine pesto.

Labeling of imported oils is not always accurate, and to date the FDA has not addressed this problem. Look for an oil that tastes of olives, without an aftertaste. When you find a good oil, buy it in small quantities. Cap it tightly and store it in a cool place.

Nuts Pine nuts, or pignolia, are a wonderful addition to the original pesto. You may prefer to toast the nuts lightly (5 minutes for pine nuts, 10 minutes for walnuts in a preheated 300°F oven).

Walnuts taste quite satisfactory in a basil pesto, but the milder pine nuts or unsalted pistachios should be used in delicate pestos, such as a tarragon or lemon pesto. Sunflower seeds and pumpkin seeds can be used in pestos also.

THE PROCESS

A handmade pesto, pounded in a mortar with a pestle, has a silky, chunky texture that cannot be duplicated in a machine. To make the traditional handmade pesto, you'll need a good-size marble mortar. Sprinkle some coarse sea salt or kosher salt and a few black peppercorns or ground black pepper from a mill into the mortar. Pound the garlic, salt, and pepper together. The coarse salt will act as an abrasive to help puree the garlic and peppercorns. Add a few pine nuts and some basil leaves with a tablespoon of olive oil and continue pounding. Stir it all up occasionally. Add more leaves and nuts and a little oil. Continue crushing and stirring and adding the nuts, herbs, and a little oil. Too much oil will make it difficult to combine the ingredients. When you have added all the nuts and basil and have a fairly smooth paste, add the freshly grated cheese and the remaining oil, a little at a time, until it is all incorporated into the pesto. You should have a thick puree. Taste for salt and season if needed. Let the pesto stand for a few minutes to allow the flavors to blend.

To make the pesto in a food processor, combine the herbs, whole garlic, grated cheese, and nuts in the bowl of the processor. Use the pulsing action to combine the ingredients. With the machine running, slowly add the olive oil. Turn the machine off, scrape down the sides of the bowl. Season to taste with salt and pepper. The texture of the pesto will be fairly coarse at this point. Continue to process until it reaches a good consistency with some texture.

Allow the pesto to stand for a few minutes to allow the flavors to develop and blend. Just before serving or using it in a recipe, retaste and add salt and pepper if needed.

Storing Pesto

Pestos will keep well in the refrigerator for 3 or 4 weeks if stored properly. Pack the pesto into a small container. Cover the pesto with a thin layer of olive oil and cap tightly. It is important to exclude as much air as possible to prevent loss of color and spoilage.

When you are ready to use the pesto, spoon out as much as you need. There will be some discoloration of the pesto on the surface, but this will not affect the flavor. Simply stir the discolored pesto into the green pesto below. Add to the top layer of oil and refrigerate the remaining pesto.

Pestos can be frozen for a year or more if packed carefully. Freeze it in small quantities to make it easy to thaw in just the amounts you need. You can freeze pesto in $1/2$-cup or 1-cup plastic containers, covered tightly. It is not necessary to cover the pesto with a layer of oil when freezing. Or, freeze the pesto, by the heaping tablespoon, on baking sheets covered with waxed paper. When the pesto is frozen, place the chunks in a plastic bag and store in the freezer.

You can also freeze plain chopped basil in olive oil in small cups or in ice cube trays. Then store the small blocks of frozen basil in plastic bags for later use. This method is a real time-saver for gardeners who raise their own basil and don't have time to make pesto for freezing.

Herb Pestos

Classic Basil Pesto   10

Red Basil Pesto   11

Basil and Oregano Pesto   12

Basil Mint Pesto   13

Pistachio Pesto   14

Lemon Pesto   15

Cilantro Pesto   16

Fennel Pesto   17

Mediterranean Pesto   18

Oregano Pesto   19

Sage Pesto   20

Tarragon Pesto   21

Creamy Tarragon Pesto   22

Thyme Pesto   23

Oregano Thyme Pesto   24

Anchovy Herb Pesto   25

Garlic Thyme Pesto   26

Classic Basil Pesto

My version of a classic basil pesto includes a small portion of Romano pecorino cheese. A true Genoese pesto usually specifies equal quantities of Sardo pecorino and Parmesan cheese. Romano pecorino, which is readily available in this country, is a much sharper cheese than Parmesan. Increasing the proportion of Parmesan to the Romano pecorino achieves a better balance of flavor.

> 2 cups loosely packed fresh basil leaves
> 2 large cloves garlic
> $1/2$ cup freshly grated Parmesan cheese
> 2 tablespoons freshly grated Romano pecorino cheese
> $1/4$ cup pine nuts or walnut halves
> $1/2$ cup olive oil
> Salt and freshly ground black pepper

Combine the basil, garlic, cheeses, and nuts in a food processor or blender. Process to mix. With the machine running, slowly add the oil. Season to taste with salt and pepper and process to the desired consistency. Let stand for 5 minutes before serving.

Makes about 1 cup

Variation: For a creamy basil pesto, replace the Romano pecorino cheese with 3 tablespoons fresh whole-milk ricotta cheese and use $1/2$ cup pine nuts or walnuts.

Red Basil Pesto

The addition of oil-packed sun-dried tomatoes to opal basil produces a pungent, intense pesto that is splendid as a sauce for pasta, fish, and fresh green beans. Sun-dried tomatoes preserved with herbs are particularly potent in this extraordinary blend.

> 1½ to 2 cups loosely packed fresh opal basil leaves
> 4 to 5 oil-packed sun-dried tomatoes, minced
>   (2½ tablespoons)
> 3 cloves garlic
> 2 tablespoons freshly grated Romano pecorino cheese
> 6 tablespoons freshly grated Parmesan cheese
> ⅓ cup pine nuts
> ½ cup olive oil
> Salt and freshly ground black pepper

Combine the basil, sun-dried tomatoes, garlic, cheeses, and pine nuts in a food processor or blender. Process to mix. With the machine running, slowly add the oil. Season to taste with salt and pepper and process to the desired consistency. Let stand for 5 minutes before serving.

Makes about 1¼ cups

Basil and Oregano Pesto

Basil and oregano combined make an interesting seasoning agent for summer vegetables, soups, and sautéed dishes. Add a little cream and Parmesan cheese to the pesto and toss with a hot pasta. Or add a little lemon juice and olive oil to dress a Greek salad.

2 cups loosely packed fresh basil leaves
3 tablespoons chopped fresh oregano
2 cloves garlic
$1/4$ cup freshly grated Parmesan cheese
$1/4$ cup walnut halves
$1/2$ cup olive oil
Salt and freshly ground black pepper

Combine the basil, oregano, garlic, cheese, and walnuts in a food processor or blender. Process to mix. With the machine running, slowly add the oil. Season to taste with salt and pepper and process to the desired consistency. Let stand for 5 minutes before serving.

Makes about 1 cup

Basil Mint Pesto

The combination of basil and mint produces a fresh sharp flavor. Freeze some to serve on the side with hearty winter soups. Or stuff into mushrooms and top with a sprinkling of bread crumbs.

    1 cup loosely packed fresh basil leaves
    1 cup loosely packed fresh mint leaves
    2 cloves garlic
    1/4 cup freshly grated Parmesan cheese
    1/4 cup pine nuts or walnut halves
    1/2 cup olive oil
    Salt and freshly ground black pepper

Combine the basil, mint, garlic, cheese, and nuts in a food processor or blender. Process to mix. With the machine running, slowly add the oil. Season to taste with salt and pepper and process to the desired consistency. Let stand for 5 minutes before serving.

Makes about 1 cup

Pistachio Pesto

Pistachio pesto is an interesting variation on the Classic Basil Pesto (page 10) and can be used interchangeably in recipes. The pistachios add a subtle nut flavor of their own. Serve it over pasta or use in any recipe specifying a basil pesto.

2 cups loosely packed fresh basil leaves
2 large cloves garlic
$1/4$ cup freshly grated Parmesan cheese
$1/3$ cup shelled unsalted pistachio nuts
$1/2$ cup olive oil
Salt and freshly ground black pepper

Combine the basil, garlic, cheese, and pistachio nuts in a food processor or blender. Process to mix. With the machine running, slowly add the oil. Season to taste with salt and pepper and process to the desired consistency. Let stand for 5 minutes before serving.

Makes about $1 1/4$ cups

Lemon Pesto

A beautiful light-green pesto that I could eat with a spoon. Double or triple this recipe; you will want some in the freezer.

> 2 cups loosely packed fresh basil leaves
> 2 large cloves garlic
> 1 tablespoon minced lemon zest
> 2 tablespoons freshly squeezed lemon juice
> $1/4$ cup pine nuts, toasted (see page 4)
> $1/4$ cup freshly grated Asiago cheese
> $1/3$ cup olive oil
> Salt and freshly ground black pepper

Combine the basil, garlic, lemon zest, lemon juice, pine nuts, and cheese in a food processor or blender. Process to mix. With the machine running, slowly add the oil. Season to taste with salt and pepper and process to the desired consistency. Let stand for 5 minutes before serving.

Makes about 1 cup

Cilantro Pesto

Cilantro, also known as fresh coriander and Chinese parsley, makes a distinctive subtle pesto with (some claim) an addictive flavor. It makes an excellent pasta sauce. Combine with butter and serve with green beans, summer squash, zucchini, or corn on the cob. Use it to make dips, salad dressings, and sauces for seafood.

> 1^1/$_2$ cups loosely packed fresh cilantro leaves, or 1 cup loosely packed fresh cilantro leaves and ^{1}/$_2$ cup loosely packed fresh flat-leaf parsley
> 1 large clove garlic
> ^{1}/$_4$ cup freshly grated Parmesan cheese
> 3 tablespoons pine nuts
> 1 teaspoon minced lime zest
> 5 tablespoons olive oil
> Salt and freshly ground black pepper

Combine the cilantro, garlic, cheese, pine nuts, and lime zest in a food processor or blender. Process to mix. With the machine running, slowly add the oil. Season to taste with salt and pepper and process to the desired consistency. Let stand for 5 minutes before serving.

Makes about ^{2}/$_3$ cup

Fennel Pesto

Fennel gives this light-green pesto a pleasant anise flavor. Add a little cream and sliced roasted red peppers to make a delightful pasta sauce.

2 tablespoons fennel seeds
1 large fennel bulb, white part only, trimmed and
    coarsely chopped
1 cup loosely packed fresh flat-leaf parsley
2 cloves garlic
$1/4$ cup freshly grated Parmesan cheese
$1/4$ cup walnut halves
$1/2$ cup olive oil
Salt and freshly ground black pepper

Cover the fennel seeds with about 1 cup hot water and set aside while you prepare the fennel bulb.

Steam the fennel bulb until softened slightly, 4 to 5 minutes. Transfer to a food processor or blender.

Drain the fennel seeds. Add the fennel seeds, parsley, garlic, cheese, and walnuts to the food processor with the fennel bulb. Process to mix. With the machine running, slowly add the oil. Season to taste with salt and pepper and process to the desired consistency. Let stand for 5 minutes before serving.

Makes about 1 $1/2$ cups

Mediterranean Pesto

Add Mediterranean Pesto to soups, fish stews, and sautéed vegetables. Baste lamb or chicken with the pesto thinned with basting juices and a little oil or wine. Or try adding a few tablespoons of the pesto to a bread recipe for an aromatic herb bread.

2 large cloves garlic
2 tablespoons chopped fresh rosemary
1 tablespoon chopped fresh thyme
1 tablespoon chopped fresh summer savory
1 tablespoon chopped fresh oregano
1 cup loosely packed fresh flat-leaf parsley
$1/3$ cup freshly grated Parmesan cheese
$1/2$ cup walnut halves
$6^1/2$ tablespoons olive oil
Salt and freshly ground black pepper

Combine the garlic, rosemary, thyme, summer savory, oregano, parsley, cheese, and walnuts in a food processor or blender. Process to mix. With the machine running, slowly add the oil. Season to taste with salt and pepper and process to the desired consistency. Let stand for 5 minutes before serving.

Makes about $3/4$ cup

Oregano Pesto

A nice summer pesto, delicious with tomatoes, zucchini, and eggplant. Add a little cream and Parmesan cheese and toss with fresh pasta. The pesto will be more flavorful if you use a good culinary variety of oregano. The low-growing Greek oregano and the higher-growing Italian oregano are the most flavorful varieties.

$^1/_2$ cup loosely packed fresh oregano
$1^1/_2$ cups loosely packed fresh flat-leaf parsley
2 large cloves garlic
$^1/_2$ cup freshly grated Parmesan cheese
$^1/_2$ cup walnut halves or pine nuts
$^1/_2$ cup olive oil
Salt and freshly ground black pepper

Combine the oregano, parsley, garlic, cheese, and nuts in a food processor or blender. Process to mix. With the machine running, slowly add the oil. Season to taste with salt and pepper and process to the desired consistency. Let stand for 5 minutes before serving.

Makes about $1^1/_4$ cups

Sage Pesto

Try Sage Pesto under the skin of chicken breasts or mix with pine nuts and fresh bread crumbs and stuff into Cornish game hens.

> $^1/_2$ cup loosely packed fresh sage leaves
> $1^1/_2$ cups loosely packed fresh flat-leaf parsley
> 2 large cloves garlic
> $^1/_2$ cup freshly grated Parmesan cheese
> $^1/_2$ cup pine nuts or walnut halves
> $^1/_2$ cup olive oil
> Salt and freshly ground black pepper

Combine the sage, parsley, garlic, cheese, and nuts in a food processor or blender. Process to mix. With the machine running, slowly add the oil. Season to taste with salt and pepper and process to the desired consistency. Let stand for 5 minutes before serving.

Makes about 1 cup

Tarragon Pesto

Tarragon makes an aromatic, versatile pesto. You can add a little cream to it and serve the sauce over fresh pasta. Or use the pesto as a base for fish sauces and salad dressings. French tarragon is far more flavorful than other varieties.

> $^1/_2$ cup loosely packed fresh tarragon leaves
> $1^1/_2$ cups loosely packed fresh flat-leaf parsley
> 2 large cloves garlic
> Scant $^1/_2$ cup freshly grated Parmesan cheese
> $^1/_2$ cup pine nuts
> $^1/_2$ cup olive oil
> Salt and freshly ground black pepper

Combine the tarragon, parsley, garlic, cheese, and pine nuts in a food processor or blender. Process to mix. With the machine running, slowly add the oil. Season to taste with salt and pepper and process to the desired consistency. Let stand for 5 minutes before serving.

Makes about 1 $^1/_4$ cups

Creamy Tarragon Pesto

This is a creamy light pesto of fresh tarragon, lemon, and walnuts. It is especially good with angel hair pasta and delicate seafood dishes, such as trout and smoked eel.

1 cup loosely packed fresh tarragon leaves
$^1/_2$ cup loosely packed fresh flat-leaf parsley
1 large clove garlic
$^1/_3$ cup freshly grated Parmesan cheese
$^1/_2$ cup walnut halves
2 tablespoons heavy cream
1 tablespoon hot water
$^1/_2$ cup olive oil
2 tablespoons freshly squeezed lemon juice
Salt and freshly ground black pepper

Combine the tarragon, parsley, garlic, cheese, walnuts, cream, and water in a food processor or blender. Process to mix. With the machine running, slowly add the oil. Add the lemon juice, and salt and pepper to taste. Process to the desired consistency. Let stand for 5 minutes before serving.

Makes about 1 cup

Thyme Pesto

Stripping the small thyme leaves from the stem is a time-consuming task, but well worth the effort for this pungent pesto. Serve over pasta with grilled summer vegetables—red and yellow bell peppers, Japanese eggplant, and plum tomatoes—or with fresh seafood and scallops.

$1/2$ cup loosely packed fresh thyme
$1^1/2$ cups loosely packed fresh flat-leaf parsley
1 large clove garlic
$1/2$ cup freshly grated Parmesan cheese
$1/2$ cup pine nuts or walnut halves
$1/2$ cup olive oil
Salt and freshly ground black pepper

Combine the thyme, parsley, garlic, cheese, and nuts in a food processor or blender. Process to mix. With the machine running, slowly add the oil. Season to taste with salt and pepper and process to the desired consistency. Let stand for 5 minutes before serving.

Makes about $1^1/4$ cups

Oregano Thyme Pesto

Oregano thyme is a lesser-known culinary thyme, but well worth cultivating for pestos. It has a pungent flavor that is quite aromatic and distinctive.

$^1/_2$ cup loosely packed fresh oregano thyme
1 cup loosely packed fresh flat-leaf parsley
2 cloves garlic
$^1/_3$ cup freshly grated Parmesan cheese
$^1/_2$ cup walnut halves
$^1/_2$ cup olive oil
Salt and freshly ground black pepper

Combine the thyme, parsley, garlic, cheese, and walnuts in a food processor or blender. Process to mix. With the machine running, slowly add the oil. Season to taste with salt and pepper and process to the desired consistency. Let stand for 5 minutes before serving.

Makes about $^3/_4$ cup

Anchovy Herb Pesto

With the addition of a little lemon juice or vinegar, this pesto makes an excellent dressing for salads and new potatoes (page 60). The strong, rich flavor is delicious with summer vegetables. Try combining this pesto with diced tomatoes and Parmesan cheese and tossing with freshly cooked pasta.

1 to 1$\frac{1}{2}$ tablespoons anchovy paste, or 6 anchovy fillets,
  patted dry and chopped
1 cup loosely packed fresh flat-leaf parsley
1 tablespoon dried oregano
1 tablespoon chopped fresh thyme
2 cloves garlic
$\frac{1}{4}$ cup freshly grated Parmesan cheese
$\frac{1}{4}$ cup walnut halves
$\frac{1}{3}$ cup olive oil
Freshly ground black pepper

Combine the anchovy paste, parsley, oregano, thyme, garlic, cheese, and walnuts in a food processor or blender. Process to mix. With the machine running, slowly add the oil. Season to taste with pepper. Let stand for 5 minutes before serving.

Makes about $\frac{3}{4}$ cup

Garlic Thyme Pesto

A base of garlic confit gives an interesting sweet flavor to this pesto. It is excellent as a base for a pasta sauce or omelet filling, or use it to flavor a calzone.

$^1/_2$ cup garlic cloves
$^1/_2$ cup olive oil
2 tablespoons chopped fresh thyme, or more to taste
$^1/_4$ cup walnut halves
2 tablespoons freshly grated Parmesan cheese
$^3/_4$ cup firmly packed coarsely chopped spinach leaves
$^1/_4$ teaspoon salt, or more to taste
Freshly ground black pepper

Simmer the garlic in the oil in a small saucepan over the lowest possible heat for about 20 minutes. Do not brown! Cool the garlic in the oil.

If using a blender, blend the garlic mixture, thyme, walnuts, and cheese to a smooth paste, scraping down the sides of the blender as needed. Add the spinach leaves, salt, and pepper to taste and blend to the desired consistency.

If using a food processor, remove the garlic from the oil, reserving the oil. Combine the garlic, thyme, walnuts, cheese, spinach, salt, and pepper to taste in the processor. Pulse briefly to combine. Then add the reserved garlic oil in a slow stream, blending to the desired consistency.

Taste for salt and pepper and herb strength. You may wish to add more thyme or salt. Let stand for at least 5 minutes before serving.

Makes about 1 cup

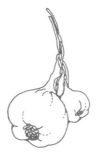

Pasta and Pestos

Vermicelli with Red Pesto   29

Artichoke and Mushroom Pasta Sauce   30

Eggplant Pasta Sauce   32

Fresh Pea and Mint Pesto Pasta Sauce   34

Sweet Red Pepper Sauce   35

Cherry Tomato Pesto Pasta Sauce   36

Fresh Tomato Shrimp Pasta Sauce   37

Pesto Pasta with Salmon Cream   38

Fresh Clam Pasta Sauce   40

Tomato Anchovy Pesto Pasta Sauce   43

Vermicelli with Red Pesto

The red pesto complements the smoked turkey beautifully, and this dish is fast to make.

- $3/4$ pound fresh vermicelli
- 3 tablespoons heavy cream
- $2/3$ cup Red Basil Pesto (page 11)
- $3/4$ cup minced smoked turkey
- Freshly grated Parmesan cheese
- 2 tablespoons very finely slivered oil-packed sun-dried tomatoes

Bring a large pot of salted water to a boil. Add the pasta, and stir with a wooden fork or spoon to separate the strands. Boil rapidly, until just barely tender. Fresh pasta cooks in 2 to 3 minutes, so check for doneness frequently. To test, lift out a piece and taste.

Stir the cream and 2 tablespoons of the hot pasta water into the pesto.

Drain the pasta and return it to the hot pan. Toss with the pesto mixture and smoked turkey. Serve garnished with Parmesan cheese and sun-dried tomatoes.

Serves 4

Artichoke and Mushroom Pasta Sauce

This is an excellent make-ahead dish. Cook the sauce and refrigerate it. Just before you wish to serve, throw angel hair pasta in boiling water and reheat the sauce. Serve with freshly grated Parmesan cheese.

> 2 tablespoons butter
> 1 shallot, sliced
> 2 (10-ounce) packages frozen artichoke hearts, thawed
>   and halved lengthwise, or 4 to 5 fresh baby artichokes,
>   quartered
> 2 tablespoons Tarragon Pesto (page 21), or more to taste
> 2 tablespoons any basil pesto (pages 10 to 15), or more
>   to taste
> 6 ounces button mushrooms, sliced (about 2 cups)
> 1 cup heavy cream
> Salt and freshly ground black pepper (optional)

Melt the butter in a large sauté pan and add the shallots. Sauté briefly over medium heat, about 2 minutes. Add the artichoke hearts and continue to sauté for 3 or 4 minutes, stirring frequently.

Stir in the pestos and the mushrooms. Add the cream, and simmer over low heat until the artichokes and mushrooms are tender and the liquid is reduced by a third, 6 to 8 minutes, stirring very little. Taste, and adjust for seasoning—adding more pesto, or salt and pepper, if needed.

Serves 4 over 1 pound of pasta

Variation: Substitute ¹/₄ cup Tarragon Pesto for the combination of half Tarragon Pesto and half basil pesto.

Eggplant Pasta Sauce

A whole-wheat pasta, such as fusilli or small shells, complement this pungent, rich eggplant sauce nicely. The sauce can be made a day ahead for a good meld of flavors. Serve over hot pasta with Parmesan cheese on the side.

$3/4$ pound small, Japanese eggplant (or substitute peeled, larger eggplant if necessary), cut into $1/2$-inch cubes ($3\,1/2$ to 4 cups)

Salt

3 tablespoons olive oil

$1/4$ cup Anchovy Herb Pesto (page 25) or Mediterranean Pesto (page 18)

4 leeks, including some light-green stem, trimmed and roughly chopped (about 2 cups)

1 ($10\,1/2$-ounce) can crushed Italian tomatoes (1 cup)

Salt and freshly ground black pepper

Sprinkle the eggplant with salt and let it drain in a colander for 30 minutes. Press out as much moisture as possible and dry in a towel.

Heat the oil and pesto in a large sauté pan over medium heat. Add the eggplant cubes and sauté, stirring frequently, for 3 to 4 minutes until softened. Add the leeks and continue to sauté over low heat. You can add a few tablespoons of water to keep the eggplant from scorching if needed and partially cover the pan. When the leeks start to become tender, after 3 or 4 minutes, add the crushed tomatoes. Cook for 3 to 5 minutes until tender but not mushy. Taste for seasoning. Serve hot.

Serves 4 over 1 pound of pasta

Fresh Pea and Mint Pesto Pasta Sauce

The success of this sauce depends on young, freshly picked peas to give the dish its sweet flavor.

> $3/4$ pound snow peas or sugar snap peas
> 2 tablespoons butter
> 3 tablespoons Basil Mint Pesto (page 13)
> 15 green onions, white part only, thinly sliced (1 cup)
> 1 cup heavy cream
> 1 cup half-and-half
> Salt and freshly ground black pepper

String the peas. Cut on the diagonal into $1/2$-inch pieces. You should have about 3 cups.

Melt the butter with 2 tablespoons of the pesto in a large sauté pan over low heat. Add the peas and green onions and sauté over medium heat until tender, about 7 minutes. Add the cream, half-and-half, and salt and pepper to taste. Reduce the heat to low and simmer until the sauce is slightly thickened, about
2 minutes. Stir in the remaining 1 tablespoon of the pesto. Taste and adjust for seasoning. Serve hot.

Serves 4 over 1 pound of pasta

Sweet Red Pepper Sauce

This mellow red sauce is delicious on pasta. I enjoy adding shrimp, squid, or chopped tomatoes and tossing with the hot pasta. The sauce also provides a perfect foil for bay scallops.

> 3 tablespoons olive oil
> 2 red bell peppers, seeded and coarsely chopped (2 cups)
> 1 onion, diced (1 cup)
> 3 tablespoons water
> 3 tablespoons Red Basil Pesto (page 11), or more to taste
> 2 tablespoons dry white wine
> Salt and freshly ground black pepper
> Pinch of cayenne (optional)

Heat the oil in a large sauté pan over medium heat. Add the peppers and onion and sauté, stirring frequently, for 4 or 5 minutes until the peppers and onion begin to soften. Add the water, cover, and simmer for 5 minutes.

Pour the sautéed vegetables into a blender or food processor and blend until smooth. Return the mixture to the pan and bring to a simmer over medium heat. Whisk in the pesto and wine. Season to taste with salt, pepper, and cayenne. You may wish to add a little more pesto. Serve hot or cold.

Makes about 1 1/2 cups

Cherry Tomato Pesto Pasta Sauce

A great-tasting tomato with a bright flavor is crucial to this dish. My favorites are the orange Sungold, Super Sweet 100, Gardener's Delight (heirloom), or a good-tasting grape tomato.

3 cups cherry tomatoes
$1/4$ cup Classic Basil Pesto (page 10)
$1/4$ cup Thyme Pesto (page 23) or Oregano Thyme Pesto
  (page 24)
1 tablespoon tarragon vinegar
1 tablespoon olive oil
Freshly ground black pepper
$1/2$ cup crumbled feta cheese, for serving
Freshly grated Parmesan cheese, for serving

Quarter the cherry tomatoes, removing the stem end as you slice.

Combine the pestos, vinegar, oil, and pepper. Taste for seasoning. Add the dressing to the tomatoes. Marinate, covered, at room temperature for at least 30 minutes. Or, refrigerate for 3 to 4 hours, then return to room temperature. Serve over hot pasta, with side dishes of feta and Parmesan cheese for sprinkling.

Serves 4 over 1 pound of pasta

Fresh Tomato Shrimp Pasta Sauce

Fresh local shrimp will provide the most flavor for this sauce. This sauce is excellent over angel hair pasta.

> 2 tablespoons olive oil
> 2 shallots, minced
> 1 pound small shrimp, peeled and deveined
> 2 large tomatoes, peeled, diced, and drained, or 1 (24-ounce)
>   can diced tomatoes, drained (2 cups)
> 4 to 6 tablespoons Oregano Thyme Pesto (page 24),
>   Thyme Pesto (page 23), or Classic Basil Pesto (page 10)
>   with 2 teaspoons chopped fresh thyme added
> 2 tablespoons chopped fresh flat-leaf parsley
> $^1/_3$ to $^1/_2$ cup crème fraîche or heavy cream
> Salt and freshly ground black pepper
> Squeeze of fresh lime or lemon juice

Heat the oil in a large sauté pan over medium heat. Add the shallots and sauté for 2 minutes. Add the shrimp and sauté for 2 minutes. Add the tomatoes and pesto. Simmer over low heat for about 3 minutes, until the juices have reduced a little. Do not overcook.

Add the parsley, crème fraîche, and salt and pepper to taste. Taste the sauce and add a little lime juice. Serve warm.

Serves 4 over 1 pound of pasta

Pesto Pasta with Salmon Cream

An excellent smoked salmon makes this dish memorable. Ducktrap River smoked salmon from Belfast, Maine (www.ducktrap.com), is a favorite— moist and lightly smoked.

3 tablespoons butter
1 large shallot, thinly sliced
1$^{1}/_{4}$ cups crème fraîche or heavy cream
Freshly ground black pepper
$^{1}/_{4}$ cup Red Basil Pesto (page 11)
$^{1}/_{4}$ pound smoked salmon, cut into $^{1}/_{4}$-inch strips
1 pound fresh linguini
Fresh opal or green basil sprigs, for garnish

Melt 2 tablespoons of the butter in a small saucepan over low heat. Add the shallots and sauté for 2 to 3 minutes until softened. Add the crème fraîche and pepper and continue to simmer for about 8 minutes until the sauce is reduced to half. Stir in the pesto and salmon.

Meanwhile, bring a large pot of salted water to a boil. Add the pasta and stir with a wooden fork or spoon to separate the strands. Boil rapidly, until just barely tender. Fresh pasta cooks in 2 to 3 minutes, so check for doneness frequently. To test, lift out a piece and taste. Drain the pasta and return to the warm pan.

Toss the pasta with the remaining 1 tablespoon butter. Divide the pasta among four warm plates and spoon the salmon cream sauce over the noodles. Garnish with basil and serve.

Serves 4

Fresh Clam Pasta Sauce

This sauce takes time to prepare, but the expense is minimal and the results are delicious. Clam juice is naturally salty, so add only pepper. I like the sauce served over an angel hair tomato-herb pasta.

Clams

   3 pounds very fresh steamer clams
   3 tablespoons chopped onion
   3 tablespoons coarsely chopped fresh flat-leaf parsley
   1 bay leaf
   $^1/_3$ cup white wine
   $^1/_4$ cup water

   $1^1/_2$ tablespoons butter
   1 carrot, finely diced ($^1/_2$ cup)
   1 onion, finely diced ($^1/_2$ cup)
   2 shallots, minced
   3 large tomatoes, peeled, diced, and drained ($1^1/_2$ cups)
   $^1/_3$ cup clam juice (cooking liquid from the clams)
   3 tablespoons heavy cream (optional)
   1 tablespoon Thyme Pesto (page 23), or more to taste
   2 tablespoons Oregano Pesto (page 19), or more to taste
   3 tablespoons chopped fresh flat-leaf parsley
   Freshly ground black pepper

Scrub and rinse the clams thoroughly. Put them in a large pot with the onion, 3 tablespoons parsley, bay leaf, wine, and water. Cover and steam over high heat for 3 or 4 minutes, just until the clams open. Remove the clams from the pot and set aside to cool a little. Strain the juices into a large measuring cup to allow the sand to settle. Discard any clams that have not opened.

Remove the clams from their shells, removing and discarding the tough neck from Eastern littleneck clams. Cover the clam meat with some of the clam broth poured carefully from the top of the measuring cup (leaving any sand on the bottom). Save $1/3$ cup clam juice. Refrigerate the clams.

Melt the butter in a large sauté pan over medium heat. Add the carrot, the onion, and the shallots and sauté until barely tender, 3 to 5 minutes, stirring frequently. Add the tomatoes and reserved clam juice, and reduce the liquids by half, cooking for about 4 minutes.

Roughly chop the clams to the size of the chopped tomatoes.

Stir the cream and the pestos into the sauté pan with the vegetables. Add the clams, chopped parsley, and pepper. Reheat for about 1 minute, but no longer, or the clams will toughen. Taste. You may wish to add more pesto. Serve hot.

Note: This dish can be partially prepared in advance. Steam the clams and remove the meat. Chop to the desired size, cover with some clam broth, and refrigerate. Save $1/3$ cup clam broth. Prepare the vegetables and refrigerate. Sauté the vegetables and clams and cook the pasta just before serving.

Serves 4 over 1 pound of pasta

Tomato Anchovy Pesto Pasta Sauce

This easy pasta sauce combines the flavors of Provence. The salt-cured olives, cultivated along the Mediterranean, are picked fully ripe and cured dry with salt. If fresh ripe tomatoes are unavailable, make the sauce with canned Italian plum tomatoes.

1¹/₂ tablespoons butter
1 Spanish onion, quartered and thinly sliced (1¹/₂ cups)
3 tablespoons Anchovy Herb Pesto (page 25), or to taste
6 to 7 plum tomatoes, peeled and sliced (2¹/₂ to 3 cups)
3 tablespoons thinly sliced salt-cured black olives
Freshly ground black pepper

In a large sauté pan, melt the butter over low heat. Sauté the onion very slowly for about 10 minutes until the onion is soft and translucent. The onion should not brown.

Add the pesto, tomatoes, and olive slices. Simmer over low heat, stirring as little as possible, for about 10 minutes, until the liquids are reduced by a third. Season to taste with pepper. Serve hot.

Serves 4 over 1 pound of pasta

For Openers:
Appetizers, Salads, and Bread

Pesto Stuffed Mushrooms   46

Red Pesto Ceviche   48

Pesto Goat Cheese Bruschetta   50

Pesto Bruschetta with Salmon   51

Crabmeat with Rosy Crème Fraîche   52

Bay Scallops with Lemon Basil Crumbs   54

Smoked Mussels with Lemon Pesto   55

Warm Goat Cheese Salad   56

Salad of Barley and Snow Peas   58

Spring Potato Asparagus Salad   60

French Country Salad   62

Tomatoes Stuffed with Pesto Pasta   64

Tabbouleh with Basil Mint Pesto   66

Artichoke and Tortellini Pesto Salad   68

Lemon Pesto Dressing   69

Anchovy Herb Dressing   70

Braided Pesto Herb Bread   71

Pesto Stuffed Mushrooms

The pesto and port wine give these mushrooms a delicious flavor, a favorite appetizer in my family for parties and holiday dinners.

> 1³/₄ pounds button mushrooms, trimmed (about 40 mushrooms)
> 3 tablespoons cold butter plus ¹/₄ cup melted
> 6 large green onions, including some green tops, minced (about ²/₃ cup)
> ¹/₄ cup Garlic Thyme Pesto (page 26)
> 3 tablespoons port wine
> 1 cup fresh bread crumbs
> ¹/₃ cup minced fresh flat-leaf parsley
> ¹/₃ cup plus 2 tablespoons grated Jarlsberg cheese (or any good Swiss-type cheese)
> 3 tablespoons freshly grated Parmesan cheese
> 3 to 4 tablespoons heavy cream
> Salt and freshly ground black pepper
> 2 to 3 tablespoons olive oil

Preheat the oven to 375 F.

Carefully break the stems from the mushroom caps and finely chop the stems.

Melt the 3 tablespoons butter in a sauté pan over medium heat. Add the green onions and mushroom stems and sauté for 3 to 4 minutes, until slightly soft. Add the pesto and the port. Simmer for about 3 minutes, until the port has reduced by half. Remove from the pan and let cool for 5 minutes.

Add the bread crumbs, parsley, and $\frac{1}{3}$ cup grated Jarlsberg and Parmesan cheeses to the pesto mixture. Add just enough cream to lightly bind the mixture together. Season to taste with salt and pepper.

Dip the outside of the mushroom caps in the melted butter and mound the stuffing lightly in the center. Top with the remaining 2 tablespoons Jarlsberg cheese and drizzle the caps lightly with olive oil. Place close together in a shallow baking dish and bake, uncovered, until just beginning to brown, about 15 to 20 minutes. Serve warm.

Serves 8 to 10

Red Pesto Ceviche

Ceviche calls for the freshest of seafood. The fish retains a tender, fresh quality because the lime juice does the "cooking." Serve as a first course or hors d'oeuvre.

- 2 pounds large shrimp, peeled and deveined, or bay or sea scallops, sliced in thirds across the grain, or a combination
- 2 teaspoons salt
- $1^1/_2$ cups freshly squeezed lime juice
- 6 to 8 large green onions, including some green tops, minced (about $^2/_3$ cup)
- $^1/_2$ cup Red Basil Pesto (page 11)
- 1 teaspoon crushed red pepper flakes
- 2 teaspoons dried oregano or 2 tablespoons minced fresh oregano
- 2 large bay leaves, crumbled
- $^1/_2$ cup olive oil
- $^1/_2$ cup sliced pimento-stuffed olives
- 2 large tomatoes, diced (about 2 cups)
- $^1/_2$ cup minced fresh flat-leaf parsley

Place the seafood in a nonreactive bowl. Add the salt, lime juice, and green onions. Stir gently to combine and refrigerate for at least 3 hours, preferably overnight.

Drain, reserving 1 cup of the marinade. Combine the reserved marinade with the pesto, red pepper flakes, oregano, bay leaves, and oil. Add to the seafood along with the olives, tomatoes, and parsley. Taste and adjust the seasoning. Serve cold.

Serves 8 to 10

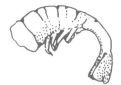

Pesto Goat Cheese Bruschetta

Bruschetta is great for a quick appetizer. The bread should be a crusty baguette with a coarse crumb. The possible toppings are many, and pesto is one of the best. Add chopped tomatoes, chopped brine- or oil-cured ripe olives, or grilled slices of Japanese eggplant or red peppers.

>   1 long crusty baguette, cut on the diagonal into 20 to
>   24 slices, $^1/_2$ inch thick
> $^1/_2$ cup olive oil
> $^1/_3$ cup any basil pesto (pages 10 to 15)
>   4 ounces soft goat cheese
>   Salt and freshly ground black pepper

Grill or broil the baguette slices, about 2 to 3 minutes on each side, until lightly toasted. Then brush each slice generously with the oil. Spread pesto on the toast and cover with a layer of soft goat cheese. Season with salt and pepper. Broil just until the cheese is warm, about 2 minutes. Serve at once.

Serves 8 to 12

Pesto Bruschetta with Salmon

Lemon Pesto and smoked salmon are a great combination, the tart lemon basil flavor blending with the savory saltiness of the salmon.

> 1 long crusty baguette, cut on the diagonal into 20 to 24 slices, $^1/_2$ inch thick
> $^1/_2$ cup olive oil
> $^1/_2$ cup Lemon Pesto (page 15)
> 4 ounces sliced smoked salmon

Grill or broil the baguette slices, about 2 to 3 minutes on each side, until lightly toasted. Then brush each slice generously with the oil. Spread pesto on each toast and top with a slice of smoked salmon. Serve at once.

Serves 8 to 12

Crabmeat with Rosy Crème Fraîche

Find the freshest crabmeat and this lovely rose-colored dish will be a knockout.

12 ounces fresh crabmeat, picked over
2 tablespoons freshly squeezed lemon or lime juice, or more
    to taste
Salt
$^{1}/_{2}$ cup crème fraîche
$^{1}/_{4}$ cup Red Basil Pesto (page 11)
Freshly ground black pepper
8 to 10 red leaf lettuce leaves (optional)
Cherry tomatoes, for garnish
Red salmon caviar, for garnish
Crackers, for serving

Toss the crabmeat gently with 1 tablespoon of the lemon juice and a little salt. Set aside.

To make the rosy crème fraîche, stir the crème fraîche into the pesto. Add the remaining 1 tablespoon lemon juice and salt and pepper. Taste for seasoning. It may need more lemon juice.

Serve the crabmeat on lettuce topped with the rosy crème fraîche. Or mound the crabmeat in a small bowl. Top with rosy crème fraîche and garnish with cherry tomatoes and red salmon caviar. Surround with crackers for a party appetizer.

Serves 8 to 10

Variation: Poach sea scallops in salted water to cover for 1 minute. Remove from heat and let cool in poaching liquid. Drain and serve with the rosy crème fraîche as you would the crabmeat.

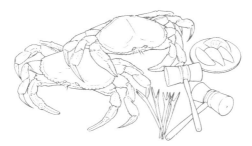

Bay Scallops with Lemon Basil Crumbs

*This dish works equally well as a first course or as a main course with a ri-
sotto and green vegetable. Accompany with a chilled light Soave and fresh
fruit for a satisfying light supper.*

  1¹/₃ pounds fresh bay scallops
  1 small lemon, halved, plus lemon wedges, for garnish
  ¹/₄ cup unsalted butter, at room temperature
  ¹/₄ cup Lemon Pesto (page 15)
  ¹/₂ to ²/₃ cup coarse dried bread crumbs (see note)
  Salt

Preheat the oven to 450° F. Lightly oil a 9 by 9-inch baking
dish. Place the scallops in a single layer in the baking dish.
Squeeze lemon juice over all.

Whisk together the butter and pesto in a small bowl. Add
enough bread crumbs to achieve a crumbly texture. Season
to taste with salt. Spoon the crumbs over the scallops and
bake until just hot and bubbly, approximately 10 minutes.
Serve hot with lemon wedges on the side.

Note: To make the crumbs, use a rustic loaf with a chewy, soft
crust, such as a ciabatta. Cube with the crusts on and process
briefly in a food processor. Dry the crumbs on a
baking sheet in a 200°F oven until dry, 10 to 15 minutes.

Serves 6 to 8 as an appetizer, 4 as an entrée

Smoked Mussels with Lemon Pesto

This is an easy appetizer that elicits much pleasure. The lemony pesto sauce complements the smokiness of the mussels beautifully.

    12 ounces smoked mussels
    $^1/_2$ cup Lemon Pesto (page 15)

In a small bowl gently combine the smoked mussels and the pesto. Serve cold with toothpicks.

Serves 8 to 10

Warm Goat Cheese Salad

This is a pesto variation of a classic California salad. The delicious, warm, soft cheese contrasts nicely with the cool greens and the tangy walnut vinaigrette. It is worth searching for a good, fresh local goat cheese, as well as a local herb vinegar and mustard.

> 5 to 6 ounces goat cheese
> 3 tablespoons Classic Basil Pesto (page 10) or
>   Mediterranean Pesto (page 18)
> 1 cup fine dried bread crumbs
> $^1/_4$ cup roughly chopped or broken walnuts, toasted
>   (see page 4)
> 1 tablespoon whole-grain mustard
> 3 tablespoons herb vinegar
> 6 tablespoons walnut oil
> Salt and freshly cracked black pepper
> $2^1/_2$ ounces baby mesclun greens
> $^1/_2$ small red bell pepper, julienned

Preheat the oven to 300 F. Lightly oil a small baking dish.

Slice the goat cheese into eight slices about $^1/_2$ inch thick. Spread both sides of the cheese with a thin layer of pesto. Dip in the bread crumbs to coat on all sides and place in the baking dish in a single layer.

Whisk together the mustard, vinegar, and oil. Season well with salt and pepper. Add the toasted walnuts. Taste and adjust for seasoning.

Reset the oven to 400°F. Bake the cheese for 8 to 10 minutes, until soft and lightly browned.

Arrange the greens and red pepper on salad plates and place two slices of warm goat cheese in the center of each. Spoon the walnut vinaigrette over all. Serve at once.

Serves 4

Salad of Barley and Snow Peas

Take this salad on a picnic with some good bread and whatever crudités are in season. As a variation, add some crumbled Montrachet or feta cheese, or a few shrimp.

3 cups water
³/₄ cup pearl barley
¹/₃ cup Anchovy Herb Pesto (page 25)
¹/₄ cup freshly squeezed lemon juice
2 tablespoons olive oil
1 tablespoon tarragon vinegar
2 teaspoons whole-grain mustard
Salt and freshly ground black pepper
2 large green onions, including some green tops,
    sliced (¹/₄ cup)
2 stalks celery, diced (about 1 cup)
¹/₃ cup broken walnuts, toasted (see page 4)
2 large tomatoes, diced (2 cups)
¹/₂ pound snow peas or sugar snap peas (2 cups)

Bring the water to a boil in a small saucepan and add the barley. Cover and simmer for about 30 minutes, until the barley is just tender. Drain and rinse with cold water. Drain well.

Whisk together the pesto, lemon juice, oil, vinegar, mustard, and salt and pepper to taste.

Combine the barley, green onions, celery, walnuts, and anchovy pesto dressing in a large bowl. Fold in the tomatoes and taste for seasoning. Chill.

String the peas and cut into $1/2$-inch pieces. Steam over boiling water for about 3 minutes. Drain and shock in cold water to stop the cooking process. Drain again and refrigerate.

Fold the pea pods into the salad just before serving. This dish can be eaten cold or at room temperature.

Serves 4

Spring Potato Asparagus Salad

Excellent smoked fish is readily available now, and the popular new smokers have made it easy for people to smoke their own catch. The red-skinned new potatoes, fresh green asparagus, and trout, combined with the green of the pesto dressing, make a colorful springtime combination. I like to serve this salad on a fish platter, garnished with red and green leaf lettuce and sunflower seed sprouts.

> $1^1/_2$ pounds new red potatoes, sliced $^1/_4$ inch thick (about 3 cups)
> $^1/_3$ cup Anchovy Herb Pesto (page 25)
> $^1/_4$ cup olive oil
> 2 tablespoons freshly squeezed lemon juice
> $1^1/_2$ tablespoons whole-grain mustard
> $1^1/_2$ tablespoons freshly grated Parmesan cheese
> 1 tablespoon tarragon vinegar
> 6 to 8 ounces smoked trout
> 1 pound asparagus, cut into $^3/_4$-inch pieces (about 2 to 3 cups)
> Salt and freshly ground black pepper

Bring 3 cups water to a boil in a medium saucepan. Add the potatoes and cook until barely tender but firm to the bite, 5 to 7 minutes. Drain the potatoes very well.

Whisk together the pesto, oil, lemon juice, mustard, cheese, and vinegar. Fold about two-thirds of the dressing into the potatoes, keeping the potatoes as whole as possible. Cover and set side.

Carefully remove the skin and small bones from the trout and break the meat into bite-size pieces approximately $3/4$-inch square. Fold into the potatoes. Chill.

Steam the asparagus over boiling water until barely tender, bright green, and crunchy, 3 to 5 minutes. Drain, shock in cold water to stop the cooking process. Drain again and chill.

Fold the asparagus into the potatoes about 30 minutes before you wish to serve the salad. Spoon the salad onto a serving platter or bowl. Pour the remaining pesto dressing over the top.

Serves 4

French Country Salad

I love cooking new potatoes and green beans together. They require the same amount of cooking time and the flavors meld beautifully. Bring sliced tomatoes and a cold white zinfandel for a picnic.

7 tablespoons olive oil
3 tablespoons Tarragon Pesto (page 21)
3 tablespoons tarragon vinegar
1 tablespoon whole-grain mustard
Salt and freshly ground black pepper
1 boneless skinless chicken breast, split
10 or 12 ounces new potatoes, sliced (2 cups)
$\frac{1}{2}$ pound fresh green beans, cut into 1-inch pieces
   ($1\frac{1}{2}$ to 2 cups)
8 or more Bibb lettuce leaves, for serving

Whisk together 6 tablespoons of the oil, the pesto, vinegar, and mustard. Season to taste with salt and pepper. Set aside.

Heat the remaining 1 tablespoon oil over medium-high heat in a medium skillet. Add the chicken and sear on both sides. Add a few tablespoons of water, partially cover, and simmer about 8 minutes, until tender. Tear the meat into bite-size pieces (about $\frac{1}{2}$ inch by 2 inches). Cover and chill.

Steam the potatoes and green beans together in a vegetable steamer over boiling water until just tender, about 6 to 8 minutes.

Combine the chicken and vegetables in a large bowl. Fold in the dressing. Marinate in the refrigerator for at least 30 minutes. Serve cold or at room temperature. Spoon the salad onto a bed of lettuce just before serving.

Serves 4

Variation: Add toasted walnuts (see page 4) for crunch.

Tomatoes Stuffed with Pesto Pasta

Beautiful summer-ripe tomatoes will make this a terrific luncheon or party dish.

- $1/4$ pound vermicelli
- 2 tablespoons Anchovy Herb Pesto (page 25)
- 1 tablespoon olive oil
- $1/2$ tablespoon freshly squeezed lemon juice
- $1/2$ tablespoon tarragon vinegar
- $1^1/2$ tablespoons pine nuts, toasted (see page 4)
- Salt and freshly ground black pepper
- 4 tomatoes of a similar size
- $2^1/2$ ounces baby mesclun greens
- 2 tablespoons crumbled goat cheese or feta cheese, for garnish

Bring a large pot of salted water to a boil. Add the vermicelli and cook over high heat until just cooked al dente. Drain well. Rinse with cold water and drain thoroughly. With a pair of kitchen scissors, cut the vermicelli into short lengths, about 2 inches long.

Whisk together the pesto, oil, lemon juice, and vinegar. In a large bowl, combine the vermicelli and dressing. Add the pine nuts and season to taste with salt and pepper.

Remove a thin slice from the stem end of each tomato.
Hollow out the centers of the tomatoes and drain upside
down for 2 minutes. Stuff the tomato shells with the pasta
and chill. Serve on mesclun garnished with the crumbled
cheese.

Serves 4

Tabbouleh with Basil Mint Pesto

With Basil Mint Pesto you can have tabbouleh in any season. Freeze the pesto in small batches so you can pull out just what you need.

> 1 1/2 cups coarse bulgur
> 3 cups boiling water
> 1 teaspoon salt
> 1/4 cup chopped fresh flat-leaf parsley
> 2 tablespoons Basil Mint Pesto (page 13), or more to taste
> 2 tablespoons olive oil
> 2 tablespoons tarragon vinegar
> 1 1/2 tablespoons freshly squeezed lemon juice
> 2 teaspoons whole-grain mustard
> 2 green onions, including some green tops, sliced (1/4 cup)
> 3 tablespoons crumbled feta cheese
> 1 cucumber, peeled, seeded, and diced, or 1/3 long seedless
>   cucumber, peeled and diced (1 cup)
> 1 large tomato, diced (1 cup)
> 1/2 head romaine lettuce, for serving
> Mint leaves, for garnish

Combine the bulgur, boiling water, and salt in a large bowl. Cover and let stand for 20 to 30 minutes, until the bulgur has softened.

Meanwhile, whisk together the parsley, pesto, oil, vinegar, lemon juice, and mustard.

Drain the bulgur well. Add the dressing, green onions, cheese, cucumber, and tomato. Mix thoroughly and refrigerate for at least 1 hour. Retaste and adjust the seasoning, adding more pesto if needed. Serve on a bed of romaine garnished with mint leaves.

Serves 4 to 6

Artichoke and Tortellini Pesto Salad

This is an easy salad to make for summer or al fresco dining.

> 1 pound frozen cheese tortellini
> $^1/_4$ cup plus 1 tablespoon olive oil
> $^1/_4$ cup Lemon Pesto (page 15), or more to taste
> 1 tablespoon tarragon vinegar or white wine vinegar
> 1 (14-ounce) can quartered artichoke hearts, drained and
> halved lengthwise ($1^1/_4$ cups)
> 1 pint grape or cherry tomatoes, halved, or 1 large tomato,
> diced (1 cup)
> 2 tablespoons minced red or green onion
> Salt and freshly ground black pepper

Bring a large pot of salted water to a boil. Add the pasta and
1 tablespoon oil and cook over high heat until al dente, 8 to
10 minutes. Drain well, rinse briefly, and drain again. Transfer
to a large bowl.

In a small bowl, whisk together the pesto, vinegar, and
remaining $^1/_4$ cup oil. Pour the dressing over the warm pasta
and toss gently. Add the artichokes, tomatoes, onion, and salt
and pepper to taste. Toss gently with two spoons. Taste again.
You may wish to add more pesto. Serve at room temperature
or chilled.

Serves 4 to 6

Lemon Pesto Dressing

Canola oil lightens this dressing. The citrus basil flavors are great with a pasta seafood salad, shrimp, or cold salmon.

$^3/_4$ cup Lemon Pesto (page 15)
$^1/_4$ cup olive oil
$^1/_4$ cup canola oil
2 tablespoons freshly squeezed lemon juice
$^1/_4$ teaspoon sea or coarse salt
Freshly ground black pepper

Whisk together the pesto, olive oil, canola oil, lemon juice, salt, and pepper to taste. Or use a blender to emulsify the ingredients into a thick sauce.

Makes about 1$^1/_4$ cups

Anchovy Herb Dressing

*Surround a small bowl of this pungent sauce with crudités as an appetizer.
Or dress lightly steamed summer squash, zucchini, and tomato with this
dressing and butter. It also makes a good salad dressing for greens, new
potatoes, and pasta.*

> $1/4$ cup Anchovy Herb Pesto (page 25)
> 2 tablespoons olive oil
> 2 tablespoons canola oil
> 2 tablespoons freshly squeezed lemon juice
> 2 teaspoons tarragon vinegar
> 2 teaspoons freshly grated Parmesan cheese (optional)
> Freshly ground black pepper
> Pinch of salt

Whisk together the pesto, olive oil, canola oil, lemon juice,
vinegar, and cheese. Season carefully with salt and pepper.

Makes about $2/3$ cup

Braided Pesto Herb Bread

This recipe has become a favorite of mine. The pesto, ricotta, mustard, and pine nuts give this unusual bread a distinctive aroma and tender, moist quality. Serve it with a hearty soup and salad on a cold day.

    2 tablespoons active dry yeast

    1 tablespoon sugar

    $^1/_2$ cup warm water

    3 cups unbleached all-purpose flour, plus more as needed

    $^1/_2$ teaspoon salt

    1 tablespoon crumbled dry sage

    $^1/_2$ cup whole-milk ricotta cheese

    6 tablespoons Mediterranean Pesto (page 18)

    1 tablespoon whole-grain mustard

    2 large eggs, plus 1 small egg

    $^1/_2$ cup chopped fresh flat-leaf parsley

    $^1/_4$ cup whole pine nuts plus 2 tablespoons chopped

In a small bowl, dissolve the yeast and the sugar in the water. Let stand until foamy and dissolved, about 5 minutes.

Insert the metal blade in the food processor and add the flour, $^1/_2$ teaspoon of the salt, sage, cheese, pesto, and mustard. Process for about 20 seconds.

Whisk the 2 large eggs and combine with the yeast mixture. With the motor running, pour the yeast mixture through the feed tube, and process until the dough is smooth and cleans the side of the bowl. If the dough is too moist to clean the sides of the bowl, add flour by the tablespoon through the feed tube until the dough forms a ball. Process for about 30 seconds to knead the dough. Add the parsley and $^1/_4$ cup whole pine nuts through the feed tube and process just to mix.

Place the dough in a lightly oiled bowl, turning to coat all sides. Cover with oiled plastic wrap and a towel. Set to rise in a warm place until the dough has doubled in bulk, 45 to 60 minutes.

Punch down the dough and knead briefly on a lightly floured board. I like to make this bread into what is called a "false plait," but it can be baked in two 4 by $8\,^1/_4$-inch loaf pans. For the plaited loaf, lightly oil a baking sheet. Roll out the dough on a lightly floured board to a rectangle measuring 9 by 13 inches. Cut $3\,^1/_2$-inch slices on a diagonal all the way up both 13-inch sides, leaving a solid 2-inch center of the dough. The slices should be about $^3/_4$ inch wide. Starting at one end, fold the slices up over the middle section of the dough, overlapping pieces and alternating sides. Tuck the ends in. Place on the baking sheet.

Make an egg wash by beating 1 small egg with the remaining $1/2$ teaspoon salt. Brush the loaf with the egg wash and sprinkle the remaining 2 tablespoons chopped pine nuts over the top.

Cover loosely with oiled plastic wrap and set in a warm place to rise until almost doubled in bulk, 30 to 40 minutes. Meanwhile, preheat the oven to 375 F.

Bake for 30 to 35 minutes, until the loaf sounds hollow when tapped. Transfer to a rack to cool. Serve warm.

Makes 1 large braided loaf or 2 medium-size loaves

Sides and Entrées

Pesto Soubise   75

Summer Vegetable Gratin   76

Mussels with Lemon Pesto   77

Pesto Frittata   78

Quick Pizza Dough   80

Grilled Pizza with Pesto, Goat Cheese,
    and Artichokes   82

Grilled Pizza with Pesto, Eggplant,
    and Red Pepper   84

Lamb Grilled with Pesto Marinade   86

Grilled Monkfish   88

Pesto Soubise

The French soubise is a perfect slow-baked combination of onions and rice, enriched with cheese and cream. The pesto adds a boost of flavor.

> $^1/_3$ cup long-grain white rice
> 2 tablespoons butter
> $^1/_2$ cup Classic Basil Pesto (page 10)
> 2 to 3 large onions, coarsely chopped (4 cups)
> Salt and freshly ground black pepper
> $^1/_4$ cup grated Swiss cheese
> $^1/_4$ cup light cream

Bring 2 quarts salted water to a rolling boil in a large saucepan. Add the rice and boil, uncovered, for exactly 5 minutes. Drain and set aside.

Preheat the oven to 325°F.

Melt the butter with the pesto in a large skillet over medium heat. Stir in the onions, rice, and salt and pepper to taste. Mix well, until all is coated with the butter-pesto mixture. Turn into a shallow 1$^1/_2$-quart baking dish. Cover tightly with heavy foil.

Bake for 40 to 50 minutes, stirring once or twice, until the rice is tender. Remove from the oven and stir in the cheese and cream. Taste and season with salt and pepper if needed. Serve warm.

Serves 4 to 6

Summer Vegetable Gratin

This summer vegetable dish is very forgiving. Add or subtract vegetables, such as eggplant, corn, green beans, or leeks, depending on availability.

> 1 yellow summer squash, cut into $1/2$-inch dice (2 cups)
> 1 zucchini, cut into $1/2$-inch dice (2 cups)
> 2 tablespoons minced red or green onion
> 1 large tomato, diced (1 cup)
> 2 tablespoons butter, melted
> 2 tablespoons Classic Basil Pesto (page 10), Cilantro Pesto
>   (page 16), or Oregano Thyme Pesto (page 24)
> Salt and freshly ground black pepper
> $1/2$ cup grated cheddar, Monterey Jack, or Fontina cheese

Steam the squash and zucchini for 5 minutes until barely tender. Combine with the onion and tomato in a bowl.

Preheat the oven to 350°F.

Combine the butter and pesto in a small bowl. Pour over the vegetables. Add salt and pepper to taste and toss lightly. Transfer to a low-sided gratin dish and cover with aluminum foil.

Bake for 20 minutes. Remove from the oven and top with the grated cheese. Bake, uncovered, until lightly browned, about 5 minutes. Serve hot.

Serves 4

Mussels with Lemon Pesto

This is nirvana for mussel lovers. Savor the broth with a mussel on the half shell. Add a loaf of crusty bread to soak up the remaining juices.

> 6 pounds mussels, scrubbed and debearded
> 6 shallots, minced
> 1 1/2 cups dry white wine or water
> 1 cup Lemon Pesto (page 15)
> 1/2 bunch fresh flat-leaf parsley, finely chopped (1/2 cup)
> Freshly ground black pepper

Discard any open mussels. Combine the shallots and wine in a large pot and bring to a slow boil over medium heat. Simmer for 2 minutes. Add the mussels, cover and increase the heat to high. When the liquid boils, reduce the heat to medium and cook for 3 to 5 minutes, until the mussels have opened.

With a large-hole spoon or skimmer remove the mussels to hot pasta dishes or soup bowls, discarding any unopened mussels. Cover the bowls with aluminum foil.

Carefully pour the broth into a saucepan, leaving behind any sand residue in the pot. Whisk in the pesto and add the parsley and pepper to taste. Heat over medium for 2 minutes until hot. Ladle the sauce over the hot mussels and serve.

Serves 4 as an entrée, 8 as an appetizer

Pesto Frittata

A frittata is my free-form lazy way to cook on a Sunday morning, but it can also be schemed out on the drive home from work for an easy supper.

Consider these for fillings—new potatoes, red or green bell peppers, broccoli, green beans, carrots, cherry tomatoes, zucchini, Canadian bacon, mushrooms, shallots, chives, parsley, fresh herbs, and, of course, pesto.

Choose any three or four ingredients. Cut the vegetables to a uniform small size. Melt a little butter with olive oil in a large sauté pan over low heat. Sauté the veggies briefly over medium heat, stirring frequently. A little minced garlic may be added. After a minute or two, add just a little water—a tablespoon or two. Partially cover the pan and steam over low heat until the vegetables are tender crisp.

Thin about 2 tablespoons of pesto (Classic Basil Pesto, page 10; Mediterranean Pesto, page 18; Oregano Pesto, page 19 and Thyme Pesto, page 23 would all be good choices) with a little warm water or cream—a teaspoon or two—and dribble the pesto sauce over the vegetables in the pan.

Beat 4 eggs and pour over the vegetables. Scatter crumbled cheese and minced herbs or parsley over all. Fresh goat cheese, feta, Monterey Jack are possible choices. Cover the frittata and place in a 325°F preheated oven for 2 or 3 minutes, or continue heating on the stove over low heat just until set.

Serve hot in wedges, garnished with fresh herbs, parsley, or salsa.

Serves 4

Quick Pizza Dough

The food processor is speedy and does the kneading for you. The addition of sun-dried tomatoes and a little whole-wheat flour makes a delicious savory crust.

3 1/2 cups unbleached all-purpose flour
1/2 cup whole-wheat flour
1 (1/4-ounce) packet quick-rising yeast
1 teaspoon salt
1/8 teaspoon sugar
1 tablespoon chopped oil-packed sun-dried tomatoes
1 cup water
1/4 cup olive oil

Combine the unbleached and whole-wheat flour, yeast, salt, and sugar in a food processor fitted with a dough blade. Process to mix, about 20 seconds. Add the sun-dried tomatoes.

In a small saucepan over medium heat, heat the water and oil to a warm temperature (about 125° F on an instant-read thermometer). With the machine running, pour the liquid slowly through the feed tube and process until the dough forms a ball. Continue processing until the dough is well kneaded, about 40 to 45 seconds.

Turn the dough onto a lightly floured surface and cover with a clean dish towel. Let rise until doubled in bulk, 30 to 45 minutes.

Generously oil five 8-inch pie tins. Pinch the dough into 5 pieces. With floured hands, pull and stretch the dough into rounds (they won't be perfect rounds) and fit into the pie tins. Brush the pizzas with olive oil. Cover and let rise in a warm place until puffy, about 20 to 30 minutes. The dough is ready now for grilling.

Makes five 7-inch pizzas

Grilled Pizza with Pesto, Goat Cheese, and Artichokes

Your friends will love baking pizza on the backyard grill. Making a couple of varieties adds to the fun. A vegetable grill rack makes it easier to remove the pizza from the grill, turn, and add the toppings.

5 Quick Pizza Dough rounds (page 80)
$1/2$ cup olive oil
4 ounces portobello mushrooms, sliced $1/4$ inch thick and halved
2 (14-ounce) cans quartered artichoke hearts, drained and halved
$1/8$ teaspoon salt
$3/4$ to 1 cup Classic Basil Pesto (page 10)
10 to 11 ounces goat cheese, crumbled
Freshly ground black pepper

Prepare the pizza dough. While the dough is rising, make a medium-hot fire in the grill. If you have a vegetable grill rack, allow it to preheat on the grill.

Heat 1 to 2 tablespoons of the oil in a large sauté pan over medium heat. Add the mushrooms, artichokes, and salt and sauté for about 4 minutes, until the mushrooms have softened and are partially cooked.

When the dough rounds are puffy, brush the tops with olive oil and carry the crusts and toppings to the grill. Lay the crusts on the grill (or the hot vegetable grill). Depending on the size of your grill, you may have to cook in batches of 2 or 3 pizzas at a time. Cover the grill and cook briefly until the underside is lightly browned, 2 to 3 minutes.

Then, either flip the crusts with tongs and quickly load the tops or, if using the vegetable grill rack, transfer the grill rack with the pizzas to a work surface. Turn the crusts with tongs. Spread the pizza rounds with the pesto. Arrange the mushrooms and artichokes over the pesto. Top with the crumbled goat cheese and pepper to taste. Sprinkle the pizza with a little olive oil. Return to the grill. Cover and grill until the undersides are lightly browned, about $1\frac{1}{2}$ to 2 minutes more. Slice in wedges and serve hot.

Serves 4 to 5

Grilled Pizza with Pesto, Eggplant, and Red Pepper

Pizza on the grill can be convivial and delicious fun. A vegetable grill rack is handy here both for grilling the eggplant and peppers and for making the pizzas.

>   5 Quick Pizza Dough rounds (page 80)
>   1 cup plus 1 tablespoon Classic Basil Pesto (page 10)
>   2 tablespoons balsamic vinegar
>   3/4 cup plus 3 tablespoons olive oil
>   3 or 4 Japanese or Thai eggplants, cut into 3/8-inch slices
>   (about 1 pound or 6 cups sliced)
>   2 red bell peppers, julienned (2 cups)
>   6 ounces crumbled feta cheese (1 1/4 cups)

Prepare the pizza dough recipe. While the dough is rising, make a medium-hot fire in the grill. Preheat a vegetable grill rack on the grill.

Combine 1 tablespoon of the pesto, vinegar, and 3/4 cup of the olive oil in a bowl. Add the eggplant and peppers and toss in the marinade. Let stand for 10 minutes. Lift the eggplant and peppers out of the marinade and grill on the vegetable grill rack, turning frequently until softened and cooked, about 5 to 8 minutes. (If you don't have a vegetable grill rack, sauté them in a frying pan on the grill).

When the dough rounds are puffy, brush the tops with 2 tablespoons of olive oil and carry the crusts and toppings to the grill. Lay the crusts on the grill or the hot vegetable grill rack. Depending on the size of your grill, you may have to cook in batches of two or three pizzas at a time. Cover the grill and cook 2 to 3 minutes until the underside is lightly browned.

Then, either flip the crusts with tongs and quickly load the tops or, if using the vegetable grill rack, transfer the grill rack with the pizzas to a work surface. Turn the crusts with tongs. Spread the pizza rounds with the remaining 1 cup pesto. Arrange the eggplants and peppers over the pesto and top with the cheese. Sprinkle the remaining 1 tablespoon olive oil over the top. Return to the grill. Cover and grill until the undersides are lightly browned, about $1^1/_2$ to 2 minutes more. Slice in wedges and serve hot.

Serves 4 to 5

Lamb Grilled with Pesto Marinade

The lemony herbal complexity of the marinade makes this shish kebab tender and delicious, my choice for summer grilling. Lamb from the leg will be the most tender, but shoulder meat can be used. Look for 4- to 6-month-old lamb.

4 tablespoons freshly squeezed lemon juice

4 tablespoons olive oil

2 tablespoons Classic Basil Pesto (page 10)

2 tablespoons Oregano Pesto (page 19)

2 tablespoons minced onion

$1/2$ teaspoon chopped fresh rosemary, or $1/4$ teaspoon dried

1 teaspoon crushed red pepper flakes

$1 1/4$ to $1 1/2$ pounds boneless lamb (from the leg), cut into 1-inch pieces

1 red or green bell pepper, cut into 1-inch pieces

1 red onion, cut into 1-inch wedges

In a medium bowl, whisk together the lemon juice, oil, basil and oregano pestos, onion, rosemary, and crushed red pepper until blended. Reserve half of the marinade for basting. Add the lamb to the remaining marinade and stir to coat. Cover and refrigerate for 30 to 45 minutes, stirring occasionally. Bring to room temperature before grilling.

Prepare a medium fire in a grill. Thread the meat onto skewers, alternating with the pepper pieces and onions. Brush the grill rack with oil to avoid sticking.

Grill the lamb 4 to 6 inches from the heat, turning and basting frequently with the reserved marinade. Test by pressing the meat with your finger. A slight sponginess and resistance indicates medium doneness in red meat. Brush again with the marinade and serve hot.

Serves 4

Grilled Monkfish

A firm-fleshed white fish, such as halibut, swordfish, scrod, or red snapper, can be substituted for the monkfish. Throw wet wood chips on the fire for added smokiness if desired.

2 tablespoons Lemon Pesto (page 15)
2 tablespoons vegetable oil
1 large green onion, including some green tops, sliced
Salt and freshly ground black pepper
1 1/2 pounds monkfish fillets, cut into 1 1/2-inch pieces
1 red bell pepper, seeded and cut into 1 1/2-inch pieces
1 green bell pepper, seeded and cut into 1 1/2-inch pieces

Whisk together the pesto, oil, and scallion in a small bowl. Season to taste with salt and pepper.

Place the monkfish in a shallow glass or nonreactive dish and cover with the marinade. Marinate for 2 to 3 hours in the refrigerator, turning the fish occasionally.

Prepare a medium fire in a grill. Skewer monkfish pieces alternately with slices of red and green peppers.

Brush the grill rack with oil to avoid sticking. Place the skewers on the grill. Grill for 6 to 8 minutes, brushing with marinade, and turning occasionally. Test a piece of fish. It should be moist and tender. Serve hot.

Serves 4 to 6